Can You See the Sun and the Moon?

T0372154

by Anne Giulieri

Look at the blue sky.

It is daytime.

Can you see the sun?

Here is the sun.

The sun is coming up.

4

The sun is going down.

The sun can look little.

6

It can look big, too.

The sun is up in the sky.

summer

The sun is down in the sky.

winter

It is daytime.

The sun is up in the sky.

Can you see the moon?

Look at the black sky.

It is night.

Can you see the moon?

The moon can look like this.

It can look like this, too.

The moon can look little.

It can look big, too.

Can you see the sun?

Can you see the moon?

Can you see the Earth, too?

sun

moon

Earth